My Book of Encouragement for Management Because Managers Are People Too

VICKIE ARNOLD

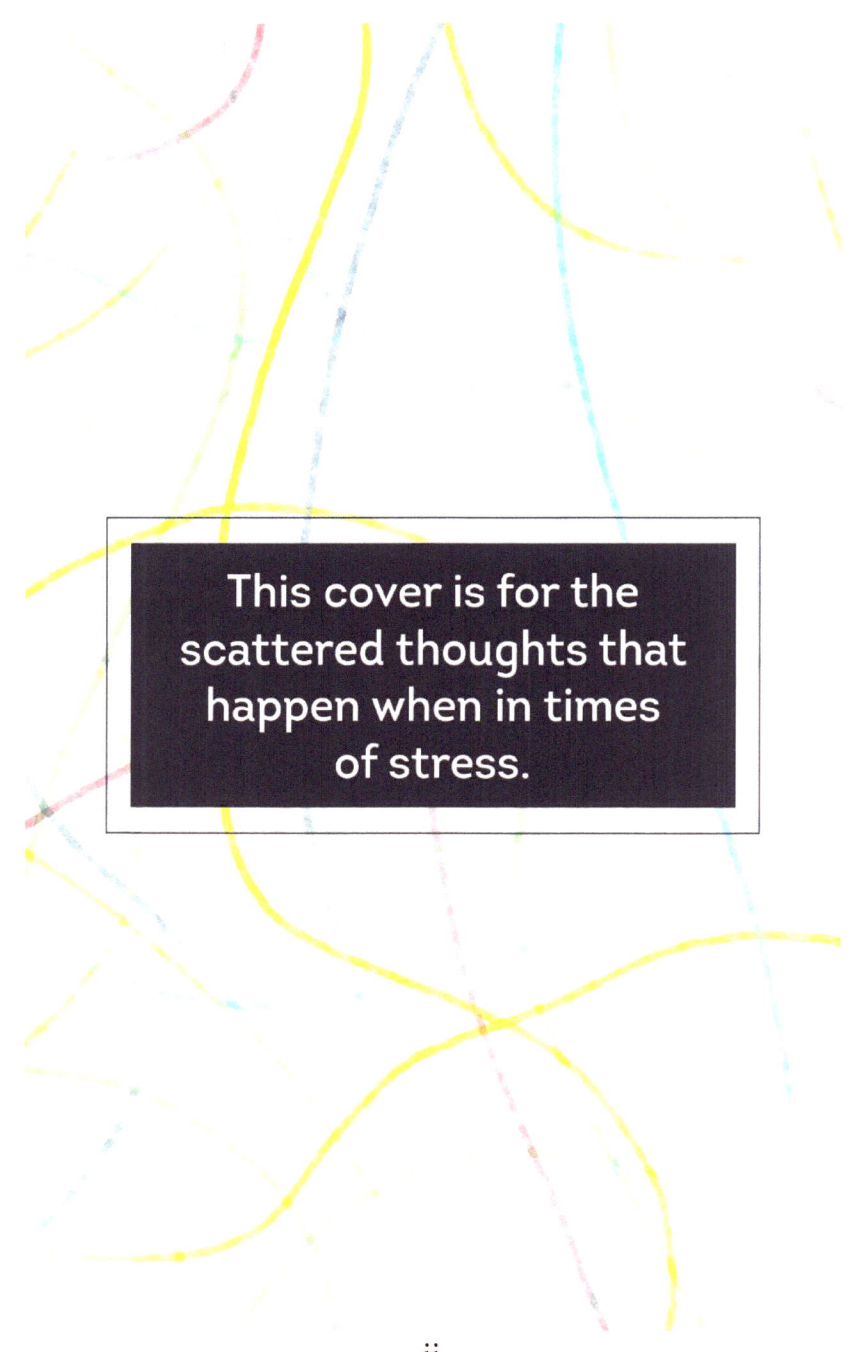

This cover is for the scattered thoughts that happen when in times of stress.

ISBN: 979-8-9854960-1-7

Dedication

This book is for all my managers that
I've had in the last eight years.
Especially my Walmart family.

CONTENTS

About the Author

I'm a wife and mother. I live in
Midland Tx. And I love to write poetry.

This page has left intentionally.

Preface

I wrote this because all of my managers have been most excellent at what they do. And always offered help no matter if it was work related or not. They were the inspiration for this book and were all wonderful friends as well.

Being Human

Try being considerate, compassionate, and understanding. That is all it takes to be human. First you must consider the feelings of the rest involved that's what starts the next step in being a good human. Then you must have compassion for the others, otherwise step one is invalid. Lastly let the understanding fly in and take over then you will be the best type of human. These are what helps everyone to feel needed. Everyone falls down from time to time let you're understanding help them be the best they can be.

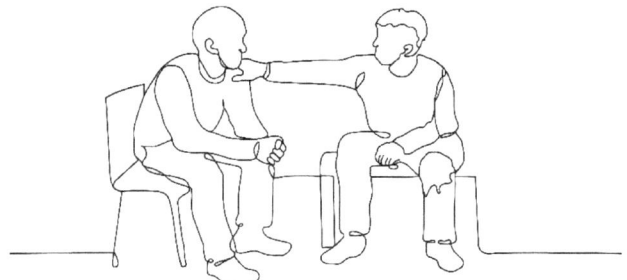

When I Change My Mindset

When the mind is clear so then is everything. Stepping back and assessing will allow this. Allow yourself to be of a clear mind set in every decision. Do what's best for everyone in the situation not just you. When this happens everyone will be happier and enjoy you more and you'll enjoy whatever you're doing more also. So in the end when the mindset changes everything gets better.

Words Matter

Whether or not meant towards one or not always make sure to be attentive to the way words being said. Words can be very powerful things they can completely destroy or on the opposite side completely energize someone. So be careful about how words are being said and how it's being understood. That's what makes a good you a good manager, person, and friend.

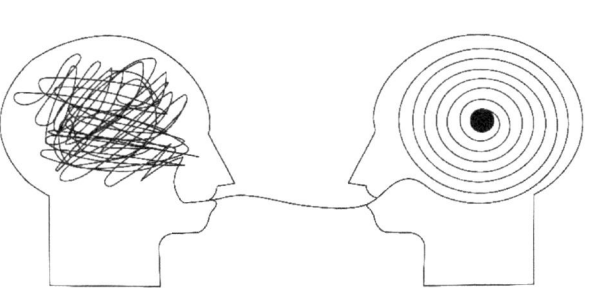

When a Person of Power Smiles

It may not mean much to you, but everything to anyone who sees it. Not only to the ones under you but also to anyone around at that moment. It shows that you are friendly and approachable. Never let it go without showing kindness. Because that's what people look for.

To Be an Inspiration

Always try to be an inspiration.

You'll always know when it's needed.

It's always from the Heart and not the mind. Never forget Heart before thinking. Never second guess your heart. That is a climb that you don't want to start. To inspirer is to pick up and speak understanding to others.

Stop to Breathe

Always remember to stop and take deep breaths for a second, so stress doesn't get the best of you. Especially at work because that's when it's important because when you're calm so will anyone under you. Because when you are calm that allows calm in everything that is going on. It's hard sometimes but don't let stress get the better of you. In doing this you'll be a better manager and person.

Things Will Be Better

Sometimes caring and understanding is all that is needed. Just stopping to see if everything is ok with everyone is the best and only thing that is needed. As a manager it's ok to not be ok but also letting people know everything will get better sometimes is all that can be said. Everyone needs to hear that every now and then. Thanks for always making sure everything was good.

Vickie Arnold

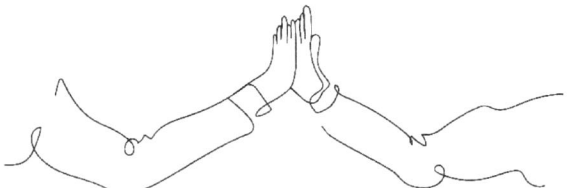

Strong is Strong

You are strong in everything you do. But especially as a manager you are the greatest no matter what anyone says. You're also a great person and friend. Thanks for just being you. Never change no matter what anyone says.

Warriors Are Needed Sometimes

Be the fierce worriers we need stand up for what you know is being done right. But at the same time be soft and kind. Because that is when your true colors will be shown.

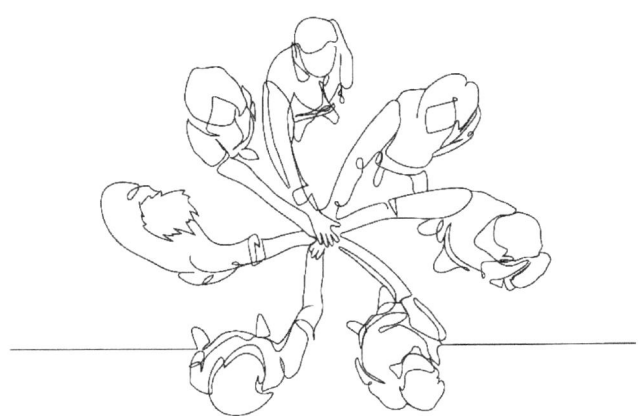

One Can't Help Everyone

As is known quite well known one can't help everyone. But when you saw a need you always asked if there was anything you could do to help. Weather work related or not you are always ready to help if necessary. Let this light always shine no matter what because sometimes that's all someone needs to know is that there is a good listener to help that won't tell anyone else.

To The Fullest

Always to the end never let the negative
moments change your compassion. There
will always be situations that are going
to test your patients but don't ever lose
your calmness, because when this happens
you lose any kind of understanding that
can be obtained. And doing so what's to
be learned from the situation will be
lost. That is why you always need to
remember to keep your compassion to the
fullest.

To Be a Fighter

Keep the fighting spirit never give up on what you believe is right. In everything you do make explosions. Because no matter what believe in what you are saying and doing. That is what it is to be a fighter. And in that you'll become a better manager, person, and friend.

My Book of Encouragement

This cover is for calm
and understanding that
I hope the pages give.